YOU CAN TEACH YOURSELF ®
RECORDER

By William Bay

A recording and a video of the music in this book are now available. The publisher strongly recommends the use of one of these resources along with the text to insure accuracy of interpretation and ease in learning.

Parts of the Recorder

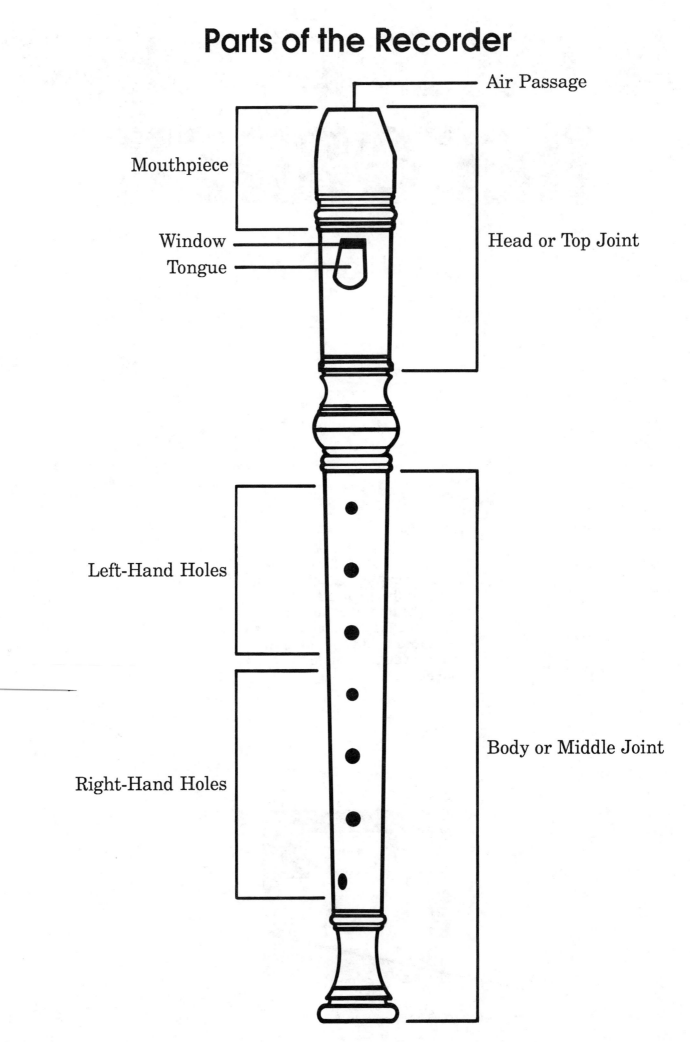

Air Passage

Mouthpiece

Head or Top Joint

Window

Tongue

Left-Hand Holes

Body or Middle Joint

Right-Hand Holes

2

Care of Your Recorder

A plastic recorder is an ideal instrument on which to begin. Later, when you have progressed in ability, you might investigate the purchase of a wooden soprano recorder. In order to keep your plastic recorder clean, run lukewarm water through it. This should be done on a regular basis. Shake off the excess water and make certain it is dry. In addition, it is a good idea to clean the mouthpiece occasionally by scrubbing it with soap.

Your local music store can sell you a recorder "swab" or a chamois. Either of these should be purchased in order to keep your recorder dry after playing. (The swab is exceptionally helpful!)

If you purchase a wooden recorder, clean it frequently with your swab and chamois. **Do not run water through it.** Keep it out of extreme hot and cold temperatures. Finally, go to your music store and purchase "cork grease." A light coating of cork grease should be spread on the cork **before** assembling your instrument each time. Remember to swab out your wooden recorder in order to dry the inside of it thoroughly before you put it away each time you have finished playing.

XIX *Flauto*

How to Hold the Recorder

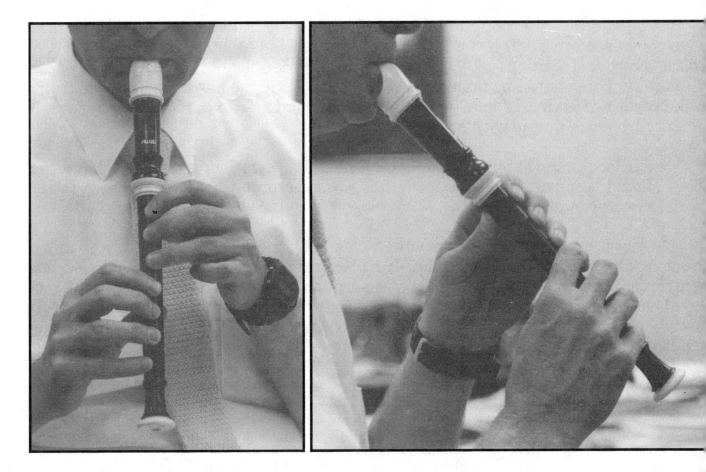

The left hand is placed above the right hand when holding the recorder. To begin with, the first finger of the left hand covers the top hole; and the left thumb covers the hole in the back of the instrument. The left middle and ring fingers cover the next two holes down from the mouthpiece. (The fleshy part of the finger is used to cover the holes.) The right-hand thumb is placed three to four inches below the left-hand thumb. Although the right thumb does not cover a hole, it helps support the recorder. The right first, middle, ring, and little fingers each cover a hole. The little finger on the right hand covers the bottom hole (which appears slightly out of line with the other holes).

The mouthpiece should be placed gently between the lips, but teeth should not actually touch the mouthpiece. Only about 1/2 inch of the mouthpiece should touch the lips. Blow gently and smoothly into the mouthpiece. The recorder is never played with hard or overly strong blowing. (That will cause a high, shrill, c squeaking sound.) Finally, make certain that your arms are relaxed and that the recorder extends down at approximately a 45° angle away from the body. Study the pictures carefully for proper positioning.

Notes

This is a note: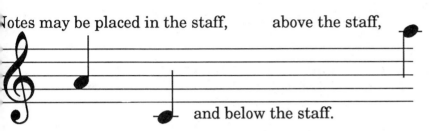

A note has three parts. They are

The HEAD

The STEM

The FLAG

Notes may be placed in the staff, above the staff,

and below the staff.

A note will bear the name of the line or space it occupies on the staff. The location of a note in, above, or below the staff will indicate the pitch.

PITCH: The height or depth of a tone.   **TONE:** A musical sound.

Types of Notes

The type of note will indicate the length of its sound.

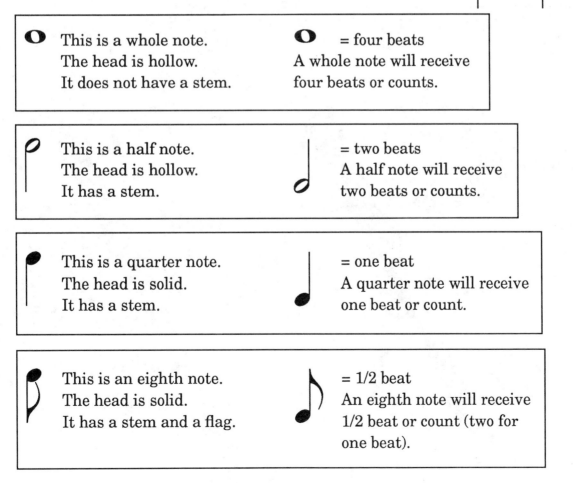

O	This is a whole note. The head is hollow. It does not have a stem.	**O** = four beats A whole note will receive four beats or counts.

	This is a half note. The head is hollow. It has a stem.	= two beats A half note will receive two beats or counts.

	This is a quarter note. The head is solid. It has a stem.	= one beat A quarter note will receive one beat or count.

	This is an eighth note. The head is solid. It has a stem and a flag.	= 1/2 beat An eighth note will receive 1/2 beat or count (two for one beat).

Rests

A REST is a sign used to designate a period of silence. This period of silence will be of the same duration of time as the note to which it corresponds.

𝄾   This is an eighth rest.   𝄽   This is a quarter rest.

▬   This is a half rest. Note that it lies on the line.

▬   This is a whole rest. Note that it hangs down from the line.

NOTES

WHOLE 4 COUNTS	HALF 2 COUNTS	QUARTER 1 COUNT	EIGHTH 2 FOR 1 COUNT
▬	▬	𝄽	𝄾

RESTS

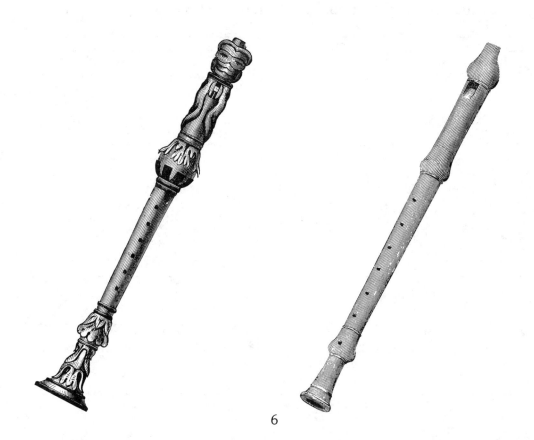

6

The Time Signature

The above examples are the common types of time signatures to be used in this book.

 The top number indicates the number of beats per measure.

The bottom number indicates the type of note receiving one beat per measure.

$\frac{4}{4}$ beats per measure.

A quarter note receives one beat.

$\frac{6}{8}$ beats per measure.

Each eighth note receives one full beat.

 Signifies so-called "common time" and is simply another way of designating 4/4 time.

Guide to Fingering Diagrams

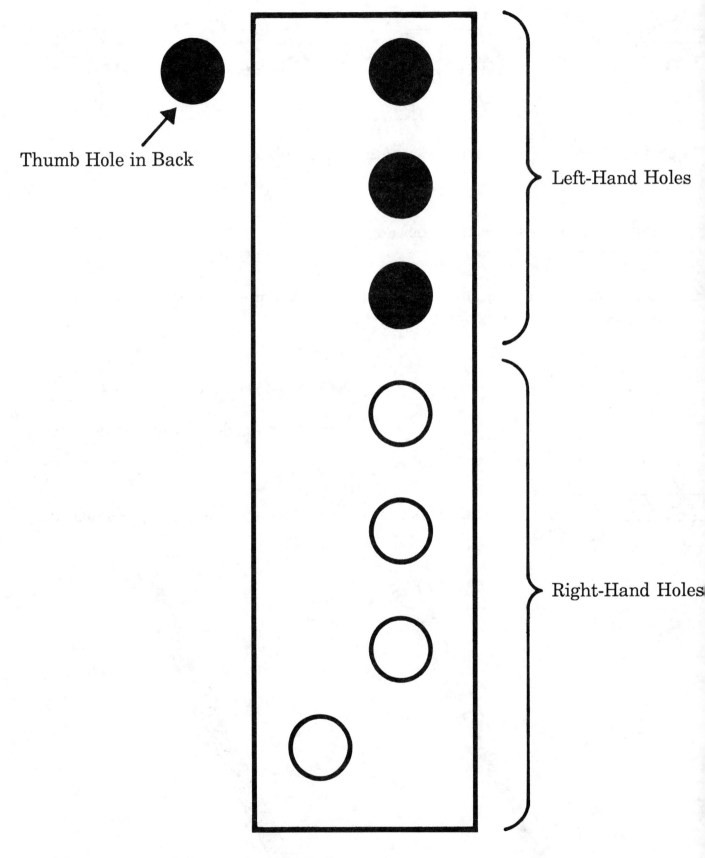

Thumb Hole in Back

Left-Hand Holes

Right-Hand Holes

● = Finger pressed down covering hole

O = Open hole (not fingered)

How to Learn a New Piece of Music

A. First look at the time signature. How many beats are there per measure?

B. Clap the rhythm while you count the note values out loud.

For Example:

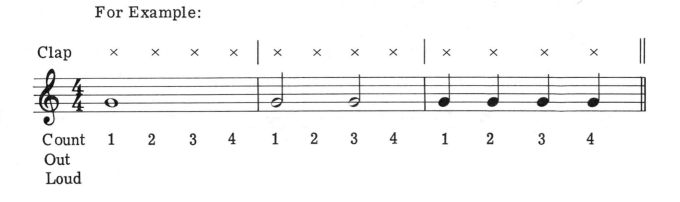

C. Finger the notes on your recorder while you count out loud.

D. Finally, play the piece on your recorder.

Our First Note

G

Studies on G

1

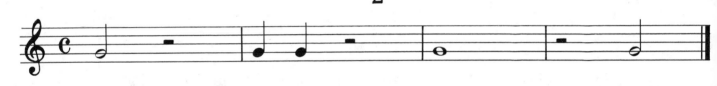

2

3

4

5

6

A

Studies on A

1

2

3

4

G and A

1

2

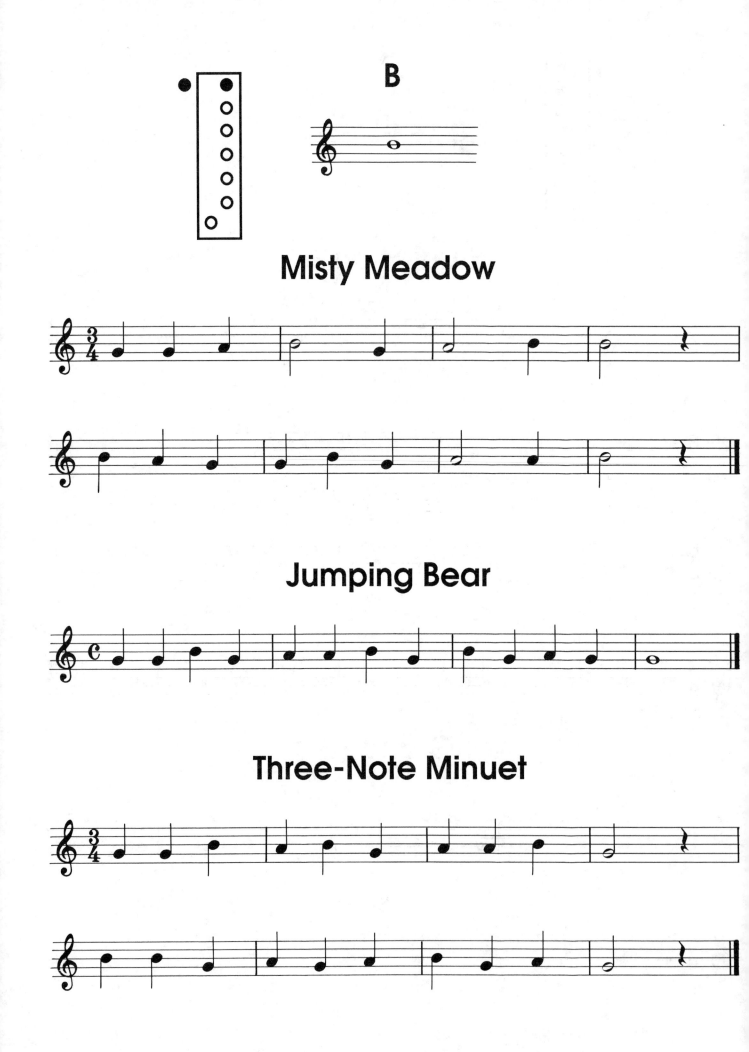

B

Misty Meadow

Jumping Bear

Three-Note Minuet

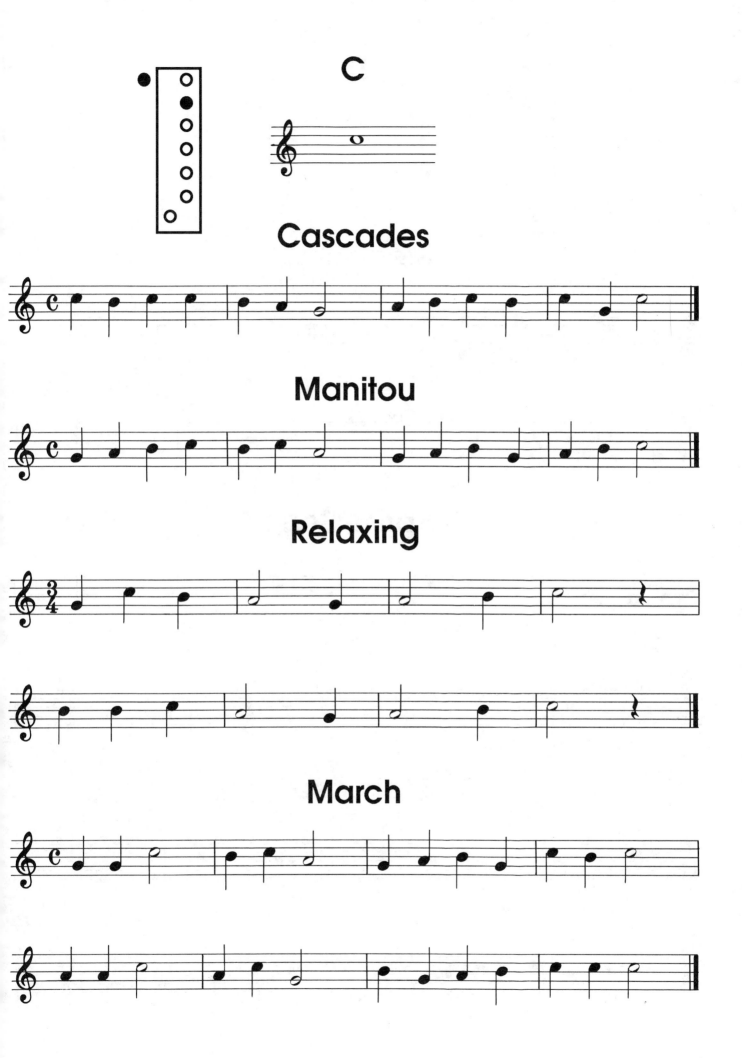

C

Cascades

Manitou

Relaxing

March

D

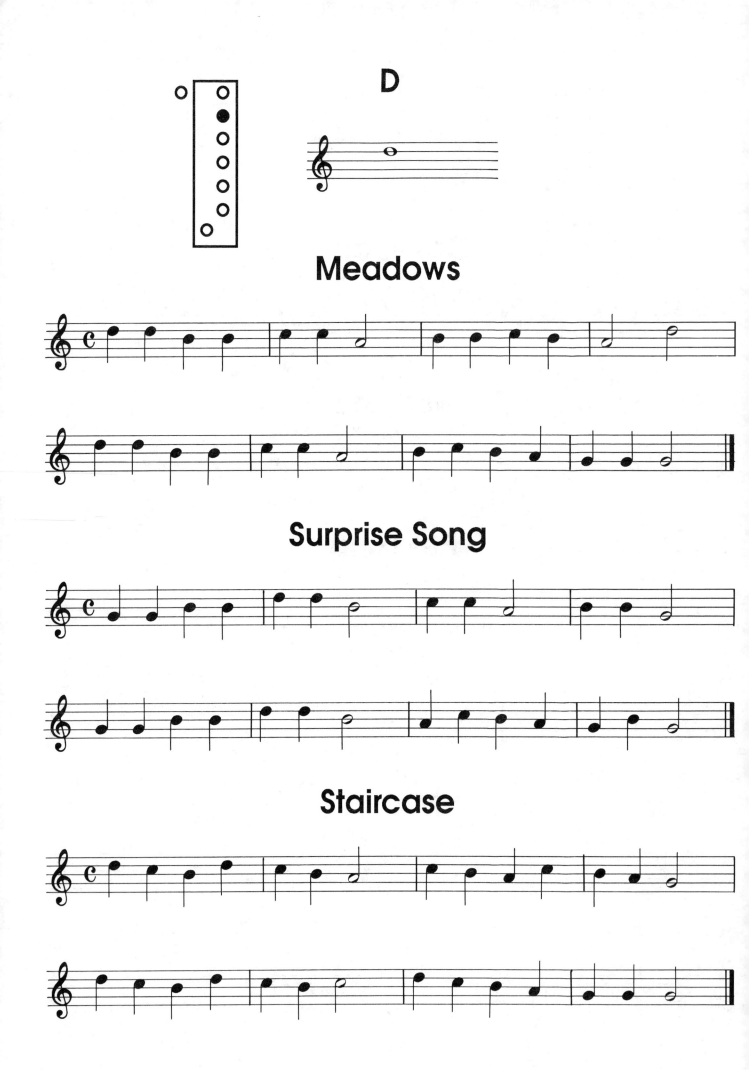

Meadows

Surprise Song

Staircase

❖ Songs to Play ❖

Ode to Joy

Beethoven

Jingle Bells

15

Dotted Half Note

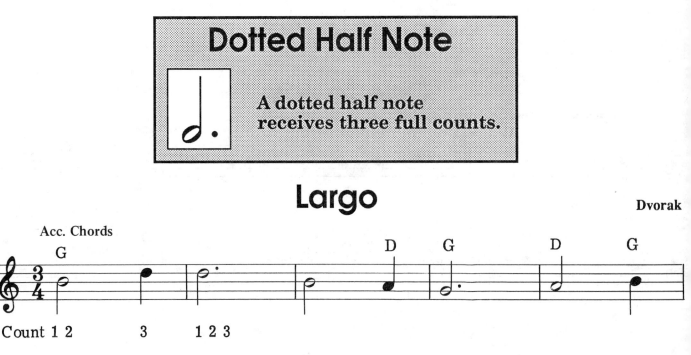

A dotted half note receives three full counts.

Largo

Dvorak

Count 1 2   3   1 2 3

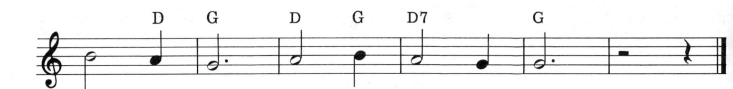

Du, Du Liegst Mir Im Herzen

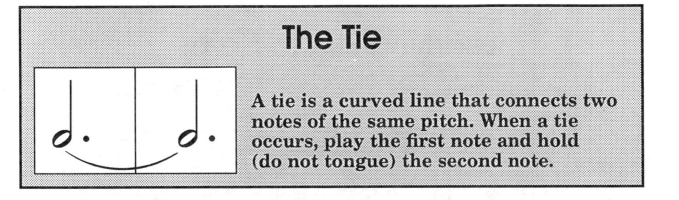

The Tie

A tie is a curved line that connects two notes of the same pitch. When a tie occurs, play the first note and hold (do not tongue) the second note.

When the Saints Go Marching In

Barcarolle
(THEME)

Offenbach

17

Learning Eighth Notes

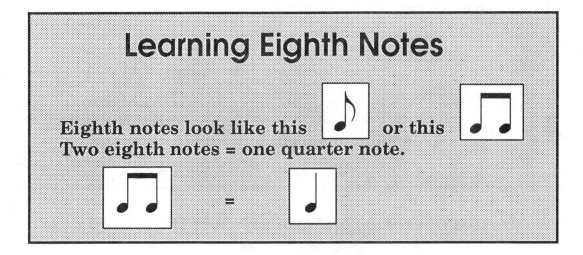

Eighth notes look like this [♪] or this [♫]
Two eighth notes = one quarter note.

[♫] = [♩]

Say and Play

Say the words to the following pieces. Clap the rhythms. Then play them on your recorder.

I Love Eating Donuts!

I love eat-ing do - nuts! I love eat-ing do - nuts!

Don't Step on Alligators

Don't step on al - li - ga-tors! Don't step on al - li - ga-tors!

Eating Pizza Makes Me Happy

Eat-ing piz-za makes me hap-py! Eat-ing piz-za makes me hap-py!

❖ Songs with Eighth Notes ❖

Renaissance Dance

Chanson

Gavotte

F

F Study #1

F March

F Study #2

F Waltz

F Study #3

E

E Study #1

Marche De Triumph

W. Bay

Eighth Rest

An eighth-note rest receives the same time value as an eighth note.

W. Bay

Count 1 & 2 & 3 & 4 &   1 & 2 & 3 & 4 &

❖ Songs to Play ❖
Wayfarin' Stranger

This piece has what is known as a "pick-up" note. A pick-up note may be only one note or a group of notes appearing before the actual start of the song. They serve to lead into the melody.

Acc. Chords

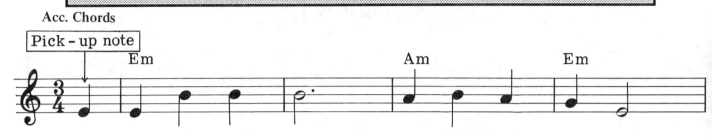

Irish Mist

W. Bay

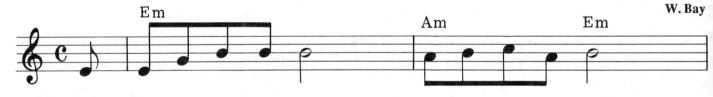

The Slur

A slur is a curved line connecting two or more notes of a __different__ pitch. When a slur occurs, tongue only the first note. The remaining notes in the slur are fingered and not tongued.

Journey

Slur Song

Once There Were Three Fishermen

Low D

D Study #1

Repeat Sign

Repeat signs look like this:

When they occur, repeat the music found between the signs.

Early American Hymn

Repeat sign—go back to beginning

Acc. Chords

G   D7   G   D7   G

G   D7   G   D7

G   D7   G   D7   G

Low C

Low C Study #1

Low C Study #2

Low C Study #3

Chester

Acc. Chords

Revolutionary War Song

25

❖ Songs to Play ❖

Scarborough Fair

Old English

Wondrous Love

Early American Hymn

Lavender Blue

English

Adore Devote

Benedictine Plainsong

Kookaburra

Children's Song

Dotted Quarter Note

A dotted quarter note receives one and a half counts.

Quarter-Note Study

Kum Ba Ya

African Hymn

Michael Row the Boat Ashore

Spiritual

Stephen Foster Song

Acc. Chords

Believe Me If All Those Endearing Charms

Irish Song

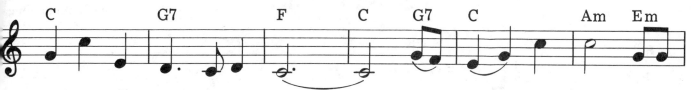

E

The thumb hole is closed only 1/2 way. This is done by pressing your left thumb nail into the hole.

E Study #1

E Study #2

Call the Ewes

Scottish Song

Acc. Chords

Dm   C   Am   G

Am   C   Dm   C   Am

Santa Lucia

Neopolitan Song

Acc. Chords

C   G7   C   A7

Dm   G7   C   Dm   G7

C   G7   C

The Ship That Never Returned

Sea Chanty

Captain Kidd

Sea Chanty

Worried Man Blues

He Is Risen

Early Christmas Morn

F

Remember that ◓ means to cover the thumb hole half way.

F Study #1

F Study #2

Morning Song

Early American
Hymn Melody

Far Above Cayuga's Waters

College Song

When I Survey the Wondrous Cross

Ancient Chant

Báidín Fheidhlimid

Irish Ballad

Dance De Mozart

W. Bay

Spanish Nights

W. Bay

The Rose of Tralee

Irish Ballad

Winds Through the Olive Trees

Hymn

❖ Songs to Play ❖

Prayer from "Finlandia"

Sibelius

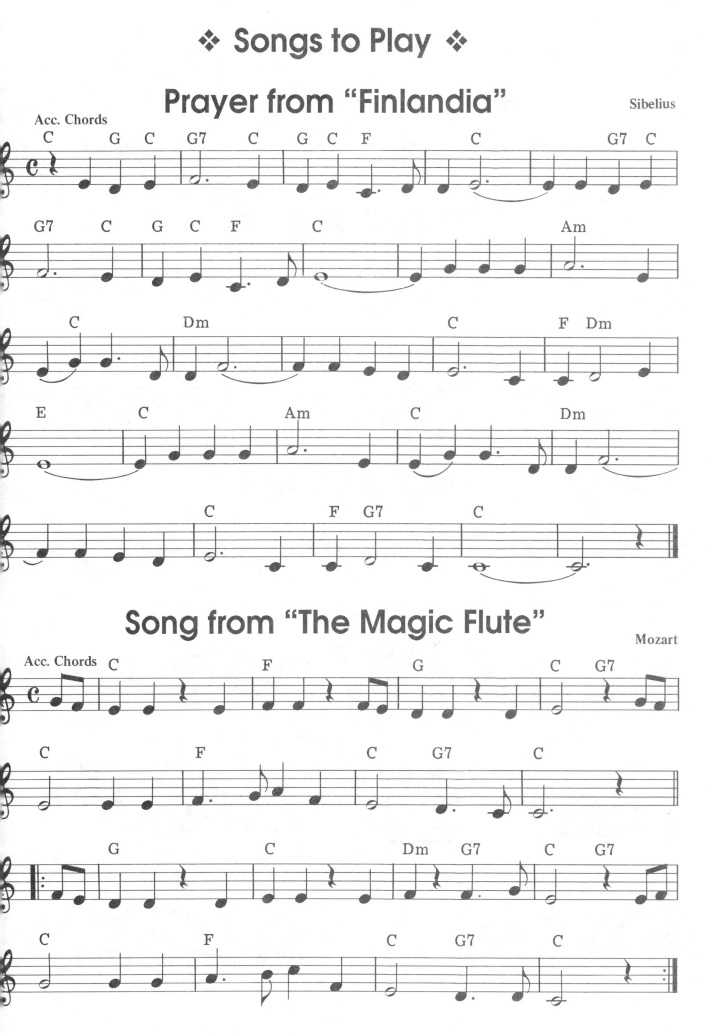

Song from "The Magic Flute"

Mozart

37

High G

High G Study #1

Marche Classique

W. Bay

Gigue

W. Bay

38

❖ Songs to Play ❖

Musetta's Waltz

Puccini

This sign is called a fermata. It means to hold the note extra long.

Tallis Canon

Thomas Tallis
16th Century

Doxology

Louis Bourgeois
16th Century

39

Grandfather's Clock

First and Second Endings

Sometimes in a song a first and second ending appear. When this occurs, take the first ending and observe the repeat sign. Then, on the second time through, skip the first ending, play the second ending, and continue on with the music. (Sometimes the song will end with the second ending.)

Folk Ballad

Chorale

Bach

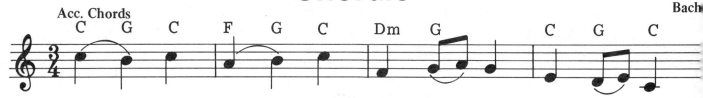

Hungarian Dance #4

Brahms

Swing Low, Sweet Chariot

41

Cockles & Mussels

Irish Melody

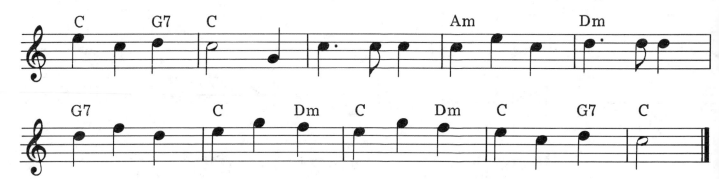

Must Jesus Bear the Cross Alone

American
Folk Hymn

The Bold Fisherman

Sea Song

Greenland Fishery

Sea Song

The Wild Rover

Irish Ballad

Precious Memories

Gospel Song

Rogue's Delight

W. Bay

Fair Lassie

W. Bay

Merlin's Fancy

W. Bay

B♭

(B Flat)

A flat (♭) lowers the pitch of a note one-half step.

B♭ Study #1

Key Signature

The key signature will appear at the beginning of a piece. It will show whether there are flats (or sharps) in a song. If a flat appears, all notes of that pitch are flatted unless cancelled by a natural sign (♮).

Fairest Lord Jesus

Key signature

Played as B♭ Because B♭ is in key signature.

F   C   F   B♭ C   F   Dm

F   B♭ F   C7   F   Dm   B♭

C   B♭   C   F   C7   F   C7   F

Juanita

(REMEMBER B♭ IN KEY SIGNATURE)

Spanish Song

Angels We Have Heard on High

47

Let All Mortal Flesh Keep Silence

17th Century French

I Will Arise & Go to Jesus

Southern American
Folk Hymn

Oh, Sinner Man

Spiritual

The Wild Colonial Boy

Irish

Simple Gifts

Shaker Song

Austrian Hymn

Haydn

Natural cancels a ♭.

God Rest Ye Merry, Gentlemen

English

F#

Low F#

High F#

A sharp (♯) raises the pitch of a note one-half step.

F♯ Study #1

Another Rule to Remember

When a sharp or flat sign occurs in a measure, all remaining notes in that measure of that particular pitch remain sharped or flatted unless a natural sign cancels the sharp or flat.

F remains sharped

F♯ Study #2

F♯ Study #3

F♯ Study #4

F♯ Study #5

German Hymn

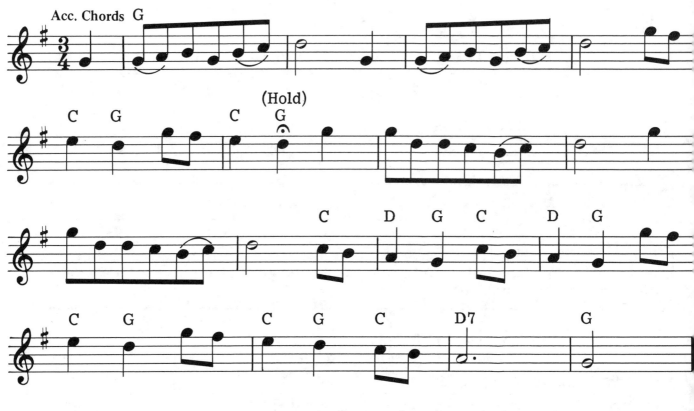

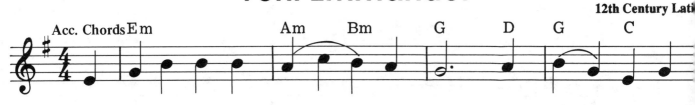

Veni Emmanuel

12th Century Latin

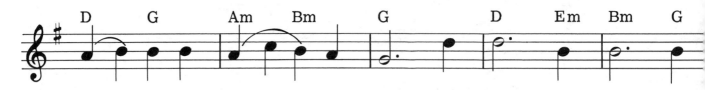

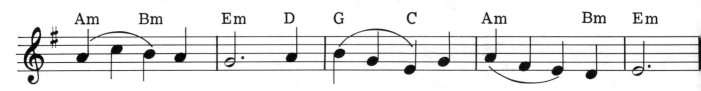

Shenandoah

American Folk Ballad

We Three Kings

Christmas Song

The Dawning of the Day

Irish Ballad

Nocturne

Mendelssohn

Coventry Carol

Old English Carol

Merry Widow Waltz

55

6/8 Time

In 6/8 time we have six beats per measure.
Each eighth note receives one full count.

6/8 Time =   Count

1   2   3   4   5   6

When Johnny Comes Marching Home

I Saw Three Ships

Traditional English

German Folk Song

High Barbaree

Sea Chanty

Irish Washerwoman

Irish Jig

The Galway Races

Irish Jig

❖ Songs to Play ❖

My Country 'Tis of Thee

French Song

Tschaikovsky

Dance

Haydn

The God of Abraham Praise

Hebrew Melody

The Ash Grove

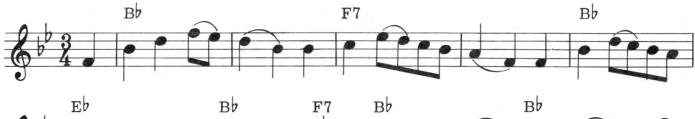

Symphony #1 Theme

Brahms

Blow Away the Morning Dew

Sea Chanty

Old Shoe Boots & Leggins

Sea Song

Sourwood Mountain

Fiddle Tune

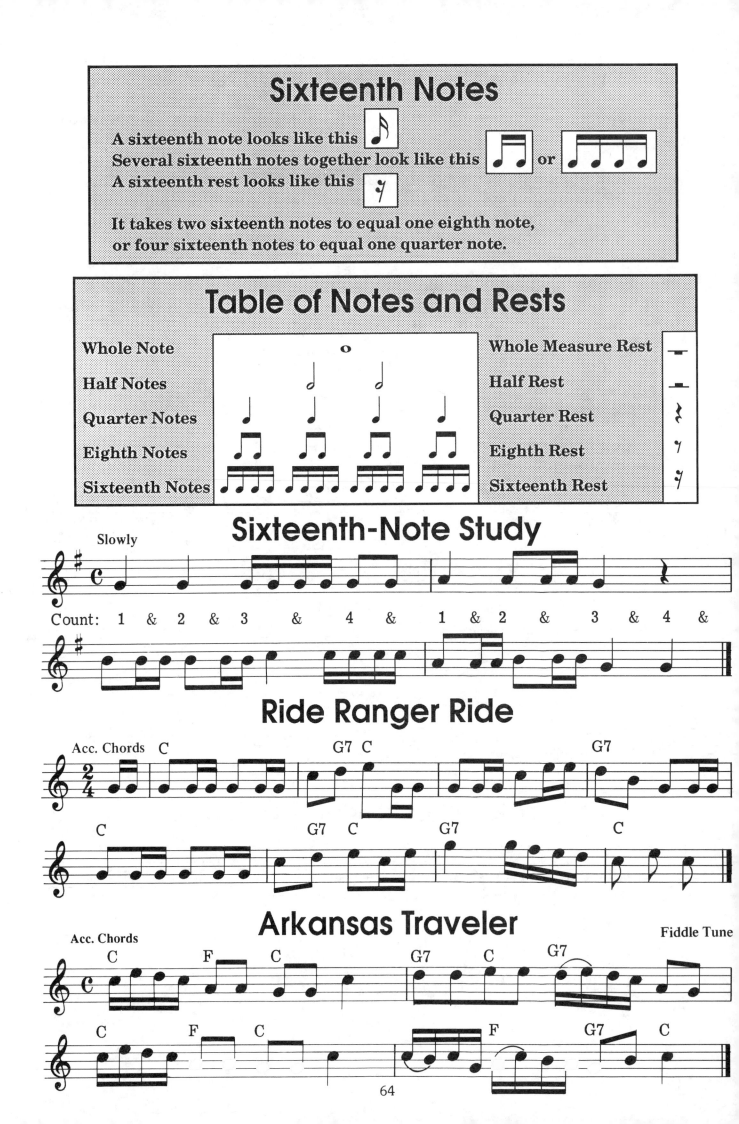

Sixteenth Notes

A sixteenth note looks like this

Several sixteenth notes together look like this or

A sixteenth rest looks like this

It takes two sixteenth notes to equal one eighth note,
or four sixteenth notes to equal one quarter note.

Table of Notes and Rests

Whole Note		Whole Measure Rest	
Half Notes		Half Rest	
Quarter Notes		Quarter Rest	
Eighth Notes		Eighth Rest	
Sixteenth Notes		Sixteenth Rest	

Sixteenth-Note Study

Slowly

Count: 1 & 2 & 3 & 4 & 1 & 2 & 3 & 4 &

Ride Ranger Ride

Acc. Chords C   G7 C   G7

C   G7 C   G7   C

Arkansas Traveler

Fiddle Tune

Acc. Chords
C   F   C   G7   C   G7

C   F   C   F   G7   C

64

Czech Marching Song

Jolly Old St. Nick

Piper's Dance

W. Bay

What Shall We Do with the Drunken Sailor?

Sea Chanty

The Wearin' of the Green

Irish

Waly, Waly

English

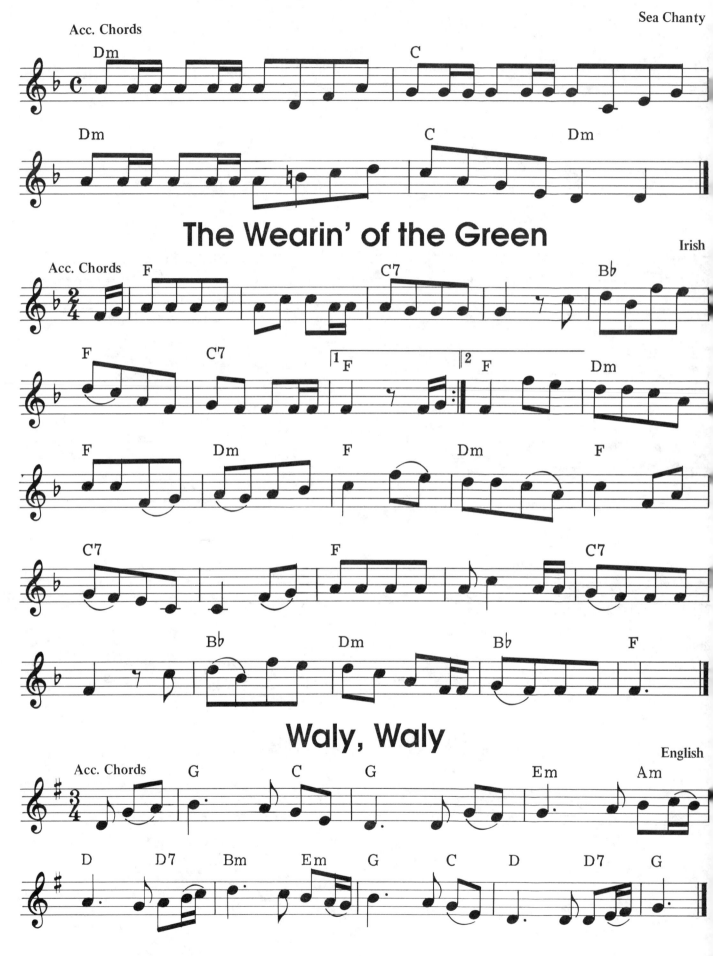

Dotted Eighths and Sixteenths

A dotted eighth note followd by a sixteenth note is a common figure in music. Practice the following study until it is felt and understood.

Study

All are Played the same

Battle Hymn of the Republic

Joy to the World

Trumpet Tune

Purcell 17th Century

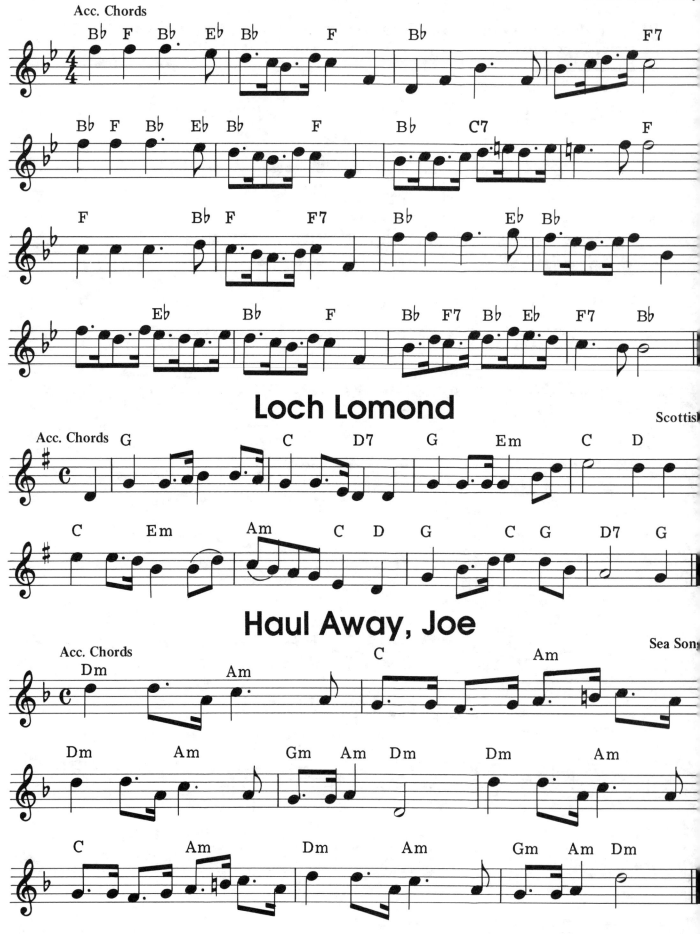

Loch Lomond

Scottish

Haul Away, Joe

Sea Song

While Shepherds Watched Their Flocks

Handel

Sail Away Ladies

Sea Song

Praise the Savior

German

69

High A

High A Study #1

Blow, Ye Winds

Early American Hymn

Londonderry Air

Irish Ballad

Haste to the Wedding

Irish Jig

El Capitan March

(THEMES)

Sousa

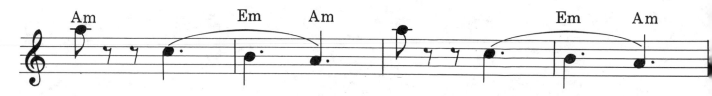

C#

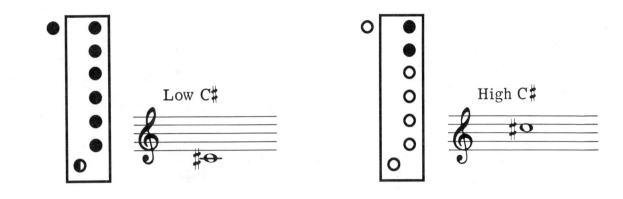

Low C# High C#

C# Study #1

C# Study #2

Notice that both F#
and C# are in the key
signature. This is
known as the key of D.

Aura Lee

American Folk Ballad

The Sally Gardens

Irish Ballad

O Sanctissima

Italian Carol

Now the Day Is Over

Hymn

The Skater's Waltz

Waldteufel

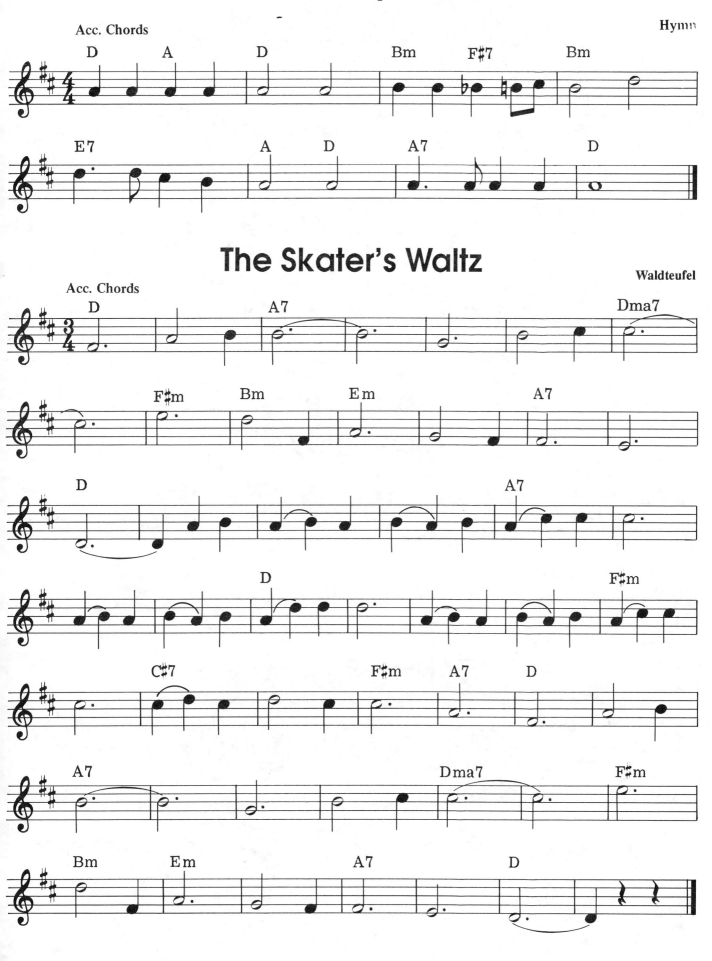

The Triplet

A triplet is a group of three notes played in the time of two notes of the same kind.

Triplet Study #1

W. Bay

Of Men & Nations

W. Bay

God of Our Fathers

March Militaire

W. Bay

Amazing Grace

(TRIPLET VERSION)

Ragtime Dance

Scott Joplin

12th Street Blues

W. Bay

"The Entertainer" Theme

Scott Joplin

Pushin' and A-Pullin' Blues

W. Bay

German Cradle Song

Fingering Chart

L. THUMB

LEFT HAND
1
2
3

RIGHT HAND
1
2
3
4

○ = open hole
● = closed hole
◑ = partly closed hole;

in case of double—hole
(3rd and 4th finger) close one hole.